Real Personal Growth for Men

A Practical Guide on Personal Development for Men Over 30

Kevin Jobson

© **Copyright 2022 - All rights reserved.**

The content contained within this book may not be reproduced, duplicated or transmitted without direct written permission from the author or the publisher.

Under no circumstances will any blame or legal responsibility be held against the publisher, or author, for any damages, reparation, or monetary loss due to the information contained within this book, either directly or indirectly.

Legal Notice:

This book is copyright protected. It is only for personal use. You cannot amend, distribute, sell, use, quote or paraphrase any part, or the content within this book, without the consent of the author or publisher.

Disclaimer Notice:

Please note the information contained within this document is for educational and entertainment purposes only. All effort has been executed to present accurate, up to date, reliable, complete information. No warranties of any kind are declared or implied. Readers acknowledge that the author is not engaged in the rendering of legal, financial, medical or professional advice. The content within this book has been derived from various sources. Please consult a licensed professional before attempting any techniques outlined in this book.

By reading this document, the reader agrees that under no circumstances is the author responsible for any losses, direct or indirect, that are incurred as a result of the use of the information contained within this document, including, but not limited to, errors, omissions, or inaccuracies.

Table of Contents

Introduction 1

Chapter 1: Your Personal Development 4

Chapter 2: Personal Development Test 11

   A Look Inside - Personal Development Test 12

Chapter 3: It Starts in the Mind 21

Chapter 4: Train Your Mind 25

Chapter 5: The Emotionally Intelligent Man 35

   The Importance of Emotional Intelligence for Men 37
   Test Your Emotional Intelligence 39

Chapter 6: Develop Emotional Intelligence 43

   Reflections and Invitations 46
   Quick Check-Ins 48

Chapter 7: Spiritual Growth 50

   Key Terms in Spiritual Development 54

Chapter 8: Spiritual Growth Exercises 58

   The Test 58
   Developing Your Spiritual Growth 59

Chapter 9: Tri-Dimensional Inner Growth 67

   Your Next Step 70
   Looking to the Future 73

Chapter 10: Revisiting Journaling 75

   Journaling Strategies 76

Conclusion 80

References 83

Introduction

Welcome to *Real Personal Growth for Men: A Practical Guide on Personal Development for Men Over 30*. I would like to welcome you on this life-changing journey. You have made the decision to take control of your life and your journey. It takes courage to try something new and open your mind to a different approach. I commend you for your willingness to learn. I am here to assist you on your journey of self-discovery and development. There are countless resources available targeted at helping us understand what it means to be men. It is easy to feel overwhelmed, even if it is difficult to admit. Once I identified that I wanted to make a change. I wanted a solution that was easy to implement. I knew that the difficulties I experienced in my journey hindered my growth. I created this guide to cut through the noise and help you identify practical strategies that create concrete change.

The idea that you have to have your life figured out by the age of 30 limited my thinking. I was a young man trying to navigate my twenties and figure out what being a man entailed. I was lost in all of the sorority talk, locker room jokes, and talks about masculinity. It worried me that manhood and masculinity are shown in a single way. I struggled with these ideas until my 30th birthday, when I decided to make a change. I want you to skip the years of exploration and grow without the unneeded stress. This is a safe space for you to express your fear, grow as a person, and discover yourself. Those concepts might be foreign to you, but I can assure you that by the end of the book, they will feel like second nature. This book is about taking control of your life and taking back your power. You are in charge of your feelings and controlling your reactions. I want you to understand the importance of emotional, spiritual, personal, and mental growth.

Self-discovery is not an unmanly trait because being a man is complex. You do not need to identify as a single thing or behave in a certain way. You should explore your masculinity and desires. I want you to open your mind and allow yourself to experience new things. This book will explore four key areas that will help you develop yourself. Each concept comes with practical easy to follow exercises to help you implement the change in your life. These initial steps will assist you in making lifelong changes. The exercises only require transparency and your willingness to learn. Do not allow yourself to live in a bubble or limit your outlook on life.

It does not matter where you are on your self-discovery journey because it is a continuous process. This book is for all men regardless of their social status, race, age, and belief system. It only requires your willingness to open yourself up to this process. The tools you learn during this process will help you tackle self-doubt and external criticisms. Similarly, it will help you accept yourself and live an authentic life. Personal development helps you grow your confidence and self-esteem. You are continuously growing and changing. Accept this growth by allowing yourself to express yourself freely.

We will examine your inner and external issues because they hold the key to your development. You must start by looking internally to assess your problem area. In order to implement sustainable change, you need to start by correcting your inner self. Once you have established inner growth, the external changes you make are less reliant on your appearance. The changes are focused on issues you have identified as opposed to the influence of others. You will learn to trust your inner voice and confidently make decisions about your life. This confidence helps you become an honorable and authentic man. Inner change bridges the gap between your outlook on life and your relationships.

We will explore everything from journaling, spirituality, and emotional intelligence to mental detoxes. Every area of your life we focus on will be accompanied by practical exercises to aid your development. Feel free to share what you learn with the men around you. This support helps you commit to this process and establish an honest dialogue around change. I want you to view this guide like a trusted friend. I am here to help you along this journey. I know that it is not an easy one, but it is necessary and effective. You are capable of altering the way you live, feel, and develop by learning to trust your instincts. I am proud of you for starting this journey at this stage of your life.

Welcome to your personal growth journey.

CHAPTER 1

Your Personal Development

Let's start with defining personal development. Defining the term will help you understand what you want to achieve. When we look at the term, it consists of two words: "personal," referring to something that belongs to you, and "development," a tangible or intangible item's ability to transform into something new. Personal development refers to your ability to transform and better yourself. This transformation takes place in every area of your life, from internal to external. When you decide to develop yourself, you are choosing to move from one level to another. Think of it as a software update on your cell phone. Before the update, your phone works just fine but not at its optimum. The update upgrades your existing software making it faster and more efficient. You would not ignore an update because you know it's important for the functioning of your device. When you update yourself you are choosing to offer the best version of yourself to the world. Similarly, a software update occurs routinely. When you ignore your updates, you are looking over your needs. Be committed to bettering yourself and consistently putting your best foot forward as opposed to walking around with outdated software. Once I looked at my needs like phone updates, I found it easier to accept the routine check I need to complete. Just like you wouldn't ignore the "check engine" signal on your car, do not ignore your inner voice.

Skipping all of the clichés, personal development is there to help you improve yourself. Personal development is just there to help you. There are countless benefits to improving yourself. You develop newfound motivation to achieve your goals. When you learn about yourself, it motivates you to find new things you enjoy, allow new experiences, and prioritize your feelings (Rolfe, n.d). Additionally, personal development is there to help you cope with stress and the different stages of your life. Understanding yourself comes with increased productivity, empathy, happiness, and improved mental health (Bundrant, n.d).

When you break it down, personal development is about giving yourself room to grow. It is an exploratory process that requires you to accept yourself. The aim is to develop an understanding of yourself that allows you to understand your triggers and needs. Personal development also allows you to fight the growing need for instant gratification. We live in a world where we are always on the go. Everything around us is constantly moving and shifting. When you understand yourself, you are allowing yourself to change with the world. This takes time and commitment to learn. You feel fulfilled as you learn more about yourself. It delays the need for instant gratification because, simply put, it takes time. Think of your growth as a special meal you are preparing. The meal requires you to pick a recipe, shop for ingredients, prepare your ingredients, and time dedicated to cooking. If it is your first time cooking, the likelihood of producing a five-star meal is unlikely. The more you practice this dish, the easier the process becomes building your confidence in your abilities.

Personal development happens in a similar manner. It requires practice and dedication. The more time and effort you put into it, the easier it becomes, allowing you to watch yourself grow.

We specify personal development for men because I want to reiterate the importance of men understanding themselves. We are not allowed to express and push ourselves. It is natural for women to work on themselves and continuously grow, but the same luxury is not given to us men. We must ignore our emotions and feelings. This limits our ability to challenge ourselves and learn. Women are praised for reflecting, bettering themselves, and showing emotion. We must also be given this opportunity. We deserve this opportunity because every person needs to understand himself or herself. I want to de-stigmatize personal development by making it accessible to all people. Growth is not limited to gender or age because, fundamentally, we all need understanding. This understanding is impactful if it starts internally. When we establish the ability to support ourselves, it gives us the opportunity to feel content. We must work on personal development because it helps every aspect of our lives. It affects your internal, personal, and professional relationships. If we are closed off to ourselves, it limits our ability to open up to others. Once you are content with yourself, it gives you the confidence to tackle any obstacle in your way.

Additionally, personal development allows you to allocate time for your needs. While "me time" is a concept that is typically geared toward women, it is for everyone. We must all dedicate time to being in our own company. The relationship you have with yourself is at the center of your interactions. Me time gives you the ability to sit with yourself and understand what makes you unique. Me time is as simple as setting time aside to do something you love. This can be five minutes to listen to music, take a walk, or watch a video. The time you allocate to yourself will gradually increase as you feel comfortable spending time with yourself. Our feelings and experiences are disguised with terms like bromances, man caves, and boys' nights. These terms give us moments to explore our masculinity. I want you to allow yourself moments to explore and express yourself outside of these limitations. It starts with wanting to get to know yourself (TheSuperiorMan, 2014).

The big question is, what does personal development specifically look like for men? It looks like allowing yourself to have new experiences, embracing your feelings, and openly expressing yourself. Men should focus on their personal relationships, inner growth, working environment, finances, and health. You should seek to develop every area of your life. You can develop every aspect of your life and challenge yourself to continuously improve. When you allow yourself to grow, you develop new goals and the opportunity to see different sides of yourself. When you develop your personal relationships, it gives you the opportunity to care for others. Personal relationships are at the center of many of our lives. We strive to be reliable fathers, partners, and relatives. When you understand the role you play in an individual's life, you strive to effectively fulfill your duties. Developing yourself allows you to be an efficient partner. Similarly, it allows you to understand what you need from your relationships. It enables you to develop the confidence to seek out meaningful relationships and trust in others. The expectations around relationship formation for men require us to continuously show our strength and assert our power. This limits our behavior and the expectations we set for our partners. Personal growth allows us to rely on others.

Secondly, personal growth enables you to advance in your professional relationships and field. Personal understanding helps you set guidelines that help you work toward your professional goals. We have all been in an unpleasant work situation with a colleague who either didn't understand us or cared to listen to anyone else's opinion. While these situations are unpleasant, they are bound to occur. Personal growth helps you develop strategies to overcome these moments. It helps you climb the professional ladder and build confidence in your skills.

A vital component of your development is your ability to acknowledge your skills and talents. It helps you identify the areas you can grow in and potentially monetize (Allegro, 2021). When I revisited my talents after years of placing them on the back burner, I rediscovered parts of myself. And rediscovering things that brought me fulfillment improved my mental health and overall happiness. Challenge yourself to do something today that once brought you joy.

Similarly, it helps you establish a work-life balance. It is easy to feel overwhelmed by your personal and professional life. You want to be successful in both fields so that you don't find yourself constantly chasing the next thing. Developing a deeper understanding of yourself allows you to escape this cycle. It gives you the freedom to take a step back and focus on your needs. This assists you in prioritizing your mental health. I know that "mental health" is a buzz-worthy term that is everywhere lately. It has gained popularity because of its importance. Your mental health is a priority because it pertains to the state of your mind. We will further explore the importance of your mental health in chapter 3. You must keep your mental state in mind when seeking to better yourself. Furthermore, you can transform areas like your finances, health, and interests through personal development. These are three areas where men are expected to thrive. Commonly, we are judged if we do not have the most money or the best body. Through personal growth, we can restructure our ideas around these areas of our lives (Rolfe, n.d).

You must start your development process more internally then more externally. The internal changes you make are the start of substantial change. Internal changes require you to accept, teach and train yourself. These changes help you continuously transform into the next stage of your life, helping you understand your fundamental beliefs, desires, and aspirations. When you examine these three areas of your life it helps you understand what motivates you. Are you working toward someone else's goals and expectations of what a man your age must achieve? Similarly, are you motivated by existing social standards? These questions help you gain perspective into the areas that you must develop. Identifying what motivates you helps increase your productivity.

Once you identify the internal changes, the external changes are easier to identify. Any insecurities or societal pressures will no longer motivate you. Personal growth allows you to be intentional about the changes you enforce, creating an environment that is conducive to long-lasting change. The internal changes you make positively affect your external interactions. They allow your career, interest, family, friends, and romantic relationships to flourish. If you do not correct an internal problem, your actions will always fall short of your expectations. If you want to succeed in every area of your life, you must display your willingness to work toward your goal. Prepare for successful finances, relationships, careers, goals, and health. Your preparations make it easier for you to work toward your goals. We will focus on three areas: your mental, emotional, and spiritual well-being. Once we lay a solid foundation and understanding of a topic, we will explore exercises that allow us to develop. Growth takes patience, a trait that is essential for every man. Be willing to be patient with yourself and your growth.

CHAPTER 2

Personal Development Test

To establish where you are on your development journey and where you need to start, we need to test your current thoughts and expectations. The test gives you a new perspective and understanding of how you currently live. It helps you assess the key areas of your life. The results will provide you with an overview of your personality, guiding you on the changes you must implement. The results are a starting point for the continuous work you must start.

The key is to start slowly and gradually progress with your growth. Do not expect drastic overnight changes but rather look for small signs that you are transforming. Each test consists of a set of questions with multiple-choice answers.

Once you have completed the test, consider your answers and establish which letter appears frequently. The letter you picked frequently indicates the areas that require your growth. Each test will indicate how frequently you should revisit the test. Look at the tests as an opportunity to check in on yourself and your feelings. Furthermore, after the multiple-choice questionnaires, there are activities to start your development process and open your mind to different perspectives.

A Look Inside - Personal Development Test

I am an...

    A - Introvert
    B - Extrovert

When I am discouraged, I tend to...

    A - Look to friends or family for support
    B - Spend time by myself
    C - Ignore the feeling

When I am sad, I tend to...

    A - Work through the emotion
    B - Talk about the feelings
    C - Disregard the feeling

When I face obstacles and disagreements, I...

    A - Try to put myself in the other person's shoes
    B - Reiterate my opinion
    C - Remove myself from the situation

I view myself as a ____ man.

    A - Kind
    B - Understanding
    C - Emotional

I want others to view me as...

    A - Strong
    B - Determined
    C - Ambitious

I enjoy listening to the opinions of others...

    A - Yes
    B - No
    C - Depends on how it can benefit me

I like to communicate my feelings through...

    A - Actions
    B - Words
    C - Only when necessary

I enjoy it when others...

    A - Listen to me
    B - Seek out my opinion
    C - Applaud me

I am detail-oriented.

    A - Yes, I enjoy focusing on detail
    B - No, I tend to look at the bigger picture
    C - I try to focus on some details depending on the importance of the task

I am concerned about the opinions of others.

    A - Yes, I care about what people have to say
    B - No, I try to not focus on what others have to say
    C - I concern myself with the opinions of the people closest to me

I apologize through...

    A - Words
    B - Actions
    C - Changed behavior

Once you have answered each question, reflect on your answers and how each question made you feel. Did you select mostly A, B, or C? The letter you selected most frequently illustrates your current behavioral patterns. If you selected mostly A, then you must focus on developing more B and C. The key is to strike a balance and develop into a well-rounded person.

A selection of mostly A illustrates that you are open-minded and reliant on others. You seek the support of others and aim to please. You are motivated by your peers and guided by your emotions. Challenge yourself to do something for yourself this week. Spend time alone and listen to your thoughts and desires.

If your selections consists predominantly of B, it reflects your reserved nature. You appreciate the comfort of others and vocalize your discomfort. You are aware of your emotions and the internal struggles you face. Challenge yourself to freely express your emotions and feelings.

Many C selections indicate that you are a closed-off man who is not open to change. You do not enjoy sharing your feelings or altering your behavior for others. Your goal is to live an autonomous life free of the opinions of others. This approach creates a barrier between you and the people around you. Challenge yourself to show your emotions and rely on others. Each set of answers has its advantages and disadvantages. Try to view your behavior holistically as opposed to limiting yourself to your habits. The goal is to implement new strategies that shape you into a well-rounded man.

Ask yourself these questions once every three months to check your progress. They will illustrate the progress you have made and help you create development goals. The defining years of your life are not in your twenties or limited to a specific period.

These questions help you look inside and gain an understanding of what makes you tick.

The following question aims to shed light on your romantic relationships. The partners you select should help you grow and develop different parts of yourself. Relationships require time and effort. That is why your partner should be worth the effort. You must feel supported and heard in your relationships. Similarly, you must provide similar support to your partner. Start by identifying what you want out of your relationship and your partner by answering these three questions:

- What three traits do I seek in a partner?
- What kind of relationships do I picture for myself?
- What does love look like for me?

These three questions are a starting point for your assessment. Once you have identified what you seek in a partner and relationships assess whether it matches up with your current behavior. Your expectations become the goals you aspire toward for your relationships. Reflect on your current behavior through the following questions:

Relationship overview

In a relationship I am...

   A – Open to criticism
   B – In control
   C – Understanding

I like it when my partner...

   A – Confides in me
   B – Relies on me
   C – Supports me

I like it when I can...

A – Provide financial support for my partner
B – Talk to my partner
C – Spend time with my partner

In a relationship, I pride myself on...

A – Honesty above all else
B - Supporting my partner
C – Sharing my feelings

In a relationship, I want to feel...

A – Protected
B – Understood
C – Secure

These questions help you understand your behavior in relationships. It is vital that you look for someone who compliments you. This is an individual with similar or compatible traits. The success of your relationship lies in your willingness to accept another individuals' differences. Additionally, reflecting on your past relationships helps you understand what you give to relationships and what they take from you. Take a moment to reflect on your past relationships and ask yourself the following question:

- Why did the relationship end?
- What did I learn from my partner?
- What was my biggest insecurity in the relationship?
- How did I show my partner that I cared?
- What mistakes did I make?
- What changes would I make to the relationship to ensure its success?
- What areas was my partner unable to provide for me?

- What challenges did we face?
- What areas was I unwilling to compromise on?
- How did my ideas around masculinity affect my relationship?

These 10 questions help you take a deep dive into your past relationships. Consider your answers while taking note of how each question makes you feel and what thoughts they produce. This process can feel draining, especially as you look at how your past relationships shaped you. Consider whether these relationships were healthy or toxic and the different ways you contributed to this.

A toxic relationship refers to an unhealthy interaction that negatively affects your mindset, self-esteem, and/or confidence. The relationship hinders your growth and creates an unhealthy tie between you and your partner. An individual seeks control over the other person's interactions and attempts to limit their behavior. The support they provide stems from a need for control as opposed to love. Toxic relationships are prone to different forms of abuse, such as emotional, physical, financial, and sexual. Reflect on your experience with these behaviors (Galla, n.d).

Once you have established what you seek and contribute to a relationship, you can begin to set realistic goals for your growth. Draft four goals for your current or future relationship. Two of the goals must show behaviors you want to develop in yourself, and the other two should focus on what you seek in a relationship. This ensures that while you develop yourself internally, you are developing your ideas around relationships.

Further, reflect on the areas that require your growth through an assessment of the people in your life. What types of people do you allow into your life, and how do these relationships affect you. Our friends and family are the people we rely on and trust. They are the people with whom we spend the majority of our time and share our feelings. Our friends and family influence our behaviors, beliefs, and mindset.

When you surround yourself with men who have unhealthy behaviors and negative mindsets you are allowing that to shape your views. Similarly, the men in your life shape your ideas around manhood. Their characters and presence shaped your views. You either molded your behaviors around what you saw or made the conscious decision to behave differently. The men you know invite you into your life are reflections of you. Be mindful of their characters and how they affect your own.

Surround yourself with like-minded men with strong values. This allows your relationships to create positive change in your life. It lets you support and rely on one another. When you embark on your development journey, the people you surround yourself with impact your progress and success. When you surround yourself with other support people who understand the importance of growth it aids your journey.

Be mindful of the people around you in every area of your life. Start by reflecting on the people who are physically in your life. How do they impact you and what does this relationship add to your life? Once you have differentiated the healthy and unhealthy interactions, you can establish boundaries in your relationships. Furthermore, assessing your virtual circle for toxic relationships and influences assists you in understanding yourself.

It is also important to identify how your social media accounts influence your behavior. Do you follow aspirational accounts, friends, and family or celebrity culture? How do those accounts make you feel? We have all encountered that one guy at the gym who wants to show off his skills. These typical gym guys either motivate us or leave us filled with jealousy. If you only interact with this gym guy once a week when you work out, it is easy to manage your relationship. If you follow this man on your social media accounts, then he begins to influence your daily mood and behavior. Do not allow those types of people and accounts to negatively affect how you view yourself.

Similarly, following accounts with unrealistic beauty standards shapes what you seek in a partner. This isn't to say that you shouldn't follow attractive people on social media or other men who inspire you. You should simply keep in mind the effect that it has on your internal view of yourself and others. Consider how it hinders or progresses your growth (Galla, n.d). Seek positive role models and people who you benefit from following. Do not underestimate the power of your social media accounts and the impact they have on your mindset. In the time you spend ideally scrolling through your accounts, you are opening yourself up to different influences.

5-minute Check-In

Sit in a comfortable place with limited distractions and set a five-minute timer. During these five minutes, write down a list of things that you are most proud of yourself for achieving. Write down the first things that come to mind, use this time to reflect on your day or week. Once you have created your list, review it and categorize the items you have written. Did you focus on personal or professional achievements? Do you consider the items on your list big or small? Lastly, how did you feel when you achieved this item? This task gives you perspective and helps you reflect on any achievements that you may have overlooked. It motivates you to work on bettering yourself and increases your confidence. Depending on your goals here are examples of potential achievements you can have on your list:

- I consistently woke up when my alarm rang.
- I went to the gym three times this week.
- I openly expressed my feelings to those around me.
- I saved on my weekly expenses.
- I prioritize my mental health.

Monthly Check-In

A monthly check-in helps you track your goals and connect to your inner needs. In this task, you are required to complete the following sentence:

This month I have achieved_____.

This simple sentence helps you track your growth and look at your life. It helps you see the progress you are making and allows you to reflect on your emotions. Similarly, tracking your goals helps you identify the areas you are neglecting.

CHAPTER 3

It Starts in the Mind

We have all heard the quotes about how powerful our minds are or the importance of a positive mindset. While these quotes can feel cliché or overused, they are correct. Your mind is a powerful tool that guides every decision you make. It is responsible for guiding your choices and influencing the outcome of your life. When you cultivate a healthy mindset, it pushes you to better yourself and confidently achieve your goals. The truth is it all starts with the mind. Take a moment to consider your mind. What do you associate with your mind? Do you think of thoughts, brainpower, mental fatigue, or maybe your memories? Your mind is at the center of your every interaction and decision. This understanding shows the importance of prioritizing your mind. When you put your mind first, you are acknowledging the role it plays in your personal development.

When you acknowledge the importance of your mind, it enables you to avoid mental slumps. A mental slump is a period where your mind is stuck in one place. Your routine begins to limit your thinking and outlook on life. A slump feels draining and counterproductive to your development. Do not allow yourself to become stuck in the same routines or activities.

Start by identifying a mental slump by remaining mindful of these signs:

- feeling overwhelmed
- lack motivation
- stuck in an unsuccessful routine
- you no longer feel fulfilled

Overcome your mental routine by noticing the signs in your life. Once you acknowledge these signs, it enables you to actively work toward changing your behavior. Start the process by giving your mind a new routine. Adding new activities into your day or completing tasks at a different time add change to your routine. Changing what you eat for breakfast or cool for dinner is a simple change that breaks you out of your routine. Do not limit your actions to set activities. When you feel trapped in your routine, it limits your growth and mind (Brown, 2022). Prioritize your mind by ensuring that you listen to your body and get a sufficient amount of sleep. Similarly, prioritize your mind by understanding the motivation behind your goals. When you work toward a goal or achievement, you must keep your mind motivated. It is common for us to lose motivation once we get a goal. This is true for our relationships, career moves, and lifestyle choices. When a partner you have been pursuing agrees to a relationship, we become complacent in the relationship. The same reasoning applies to our career goals and lifestyle changes. The moment we reach a goal, we lose our motivation. Challenge your mind by remembering the motivation behind your goals. When you keep your mind focused on what you seek to achieve, you avoid mental slumps and unproductive behaviors.

Shift your mindset around the routines that form in your professional and personal life. When we feel limited by our routines, it lowers our productivity and leads to stress. Shift your professional routine by creating a to-do list. To-do lists help your mind focus on the tasks you want to complete. Shift your work routine by writing a list of the tasks that require your attention. Challenge yourself to complete your list in a new order. This helps you optimize your productivity and keeps your work exciting. Take a similar approach to every area of your romantic relationships. Bring excitement into the everyday aspects of your relationship by surpassing your partner and openly communicating about your desires (Laderer, 2019). This allows you to develop a healthy mindset and openly express yourself.

A determined mindset makes it possible for you to achieve any goal you set for yourself. A strong mindset is a part of your journey to success. When you are certain of your abilities, you develop genuine self-esteem and confidence in yourself. When you develop the ability to overcome your negative thoughts and feelings, it puts you in charge of your future. You struggle to reach success when you limit yourself through your thoughts. When you support yourself, you can confidently try new things and grow as an individual. You must support yourself in your journey to manhood because you truly know yourself.

Develop a strong mindset by developing two traits: mental toughness and resilience. Mental toughness refers to the durability and strength of your mind. Hardships or obstacles do not deter a mentally tough person, but rather, they motivate them. Mental toughness helps you feel motivated and develop perseverance. Resilience refers to your ability to remain motivated when you face adversity. A resilient person understands that the problems they face are opportunities to learn and develop (Merriam-Webster, n.d.). Resilience differs from mental toughness because it is developed through adversity. Mental toughness is a result of this development.

Mental toughness looks different for each person, depending on your goals. Develop mental toughness by creating small goals and building your confidence. Build your toughness by creating healthy habits (Clear, n.d). Developing a firm understanding of yourself helps you identify your mental toughness. When you are mindful, it aids your personal development. Mental toughness and resilience can be developed over time.

Develop resilience through honest reflections and practicality. When you are practical about the obstacles you face, it helps you overcome them. It brings the needed awareness that the issues you face are manageable. Similarly, understanding the importance of hope helps you stay focused on your goals and develop resilience (Mental Toughness Partners, 2017). A strong mindset allows you to provide yourself with honest support because you are aware of your fears, weakness, and desires. You understand the work that you require to achieve your goals. Prioritizing your mind allows you to propel yourself to a successful life. The support you provide yourself gives you the ability to reach your goals. This is evident in many success stories. People like Tom Cruise, Tom Brady, and Michael Jordan are examples of the power of mental strength. These stories are not unique to celebrities; real people show their mental strength to overcome poverty, illness, and hardships. When you believe in your capabilities, it gives you the drive to overcome anything that you face. Strengthen your mental agility through the mindset enrichment activities in the following chapter.

CHAPTER 4

Train Your Mind

Now that you understand the importance of your mind, it is time to train yourself to develop healthy ways of thinking. You must understand your mind and the power it holds in your interactions. Once you understand your mind, it gives you the ability to further control your emotions and monitor your behavior. It increases your awareness of your triggers and helps you manage your feelings. We will focus on easy-to-follow practical exercises that will shift your mindset and train your thinking. Similarly, to develop your muscles at the gym or consistently read to develop a new skill, you must train your mind. The goal is to create new healthy habits that you can maintain.

<u>Journaling</u>

Journaling is an age-old practice that helps people manage and track their thoughts. Journaling is the simple act of writing down your thoughts and feelings. This mental exercise helps you declutter your mind by helping you pour out your thoughts.

Think of your mind like a laundry basket. When the basket is empty, it is easy to store your dirty clothes. Gradually the clothing you put into the basket begins to fill up the space. Once the basket is full, you begin to cram clothing into the basket. This is similar to your mind if you do not have an outlet for your thoughts, you begin to cram them into your mind. This causes you to feel stressed and overwhelmed.

Journaling allows you to empty your mental laundry basket and create space for new thoughts. Similarly, journaling helps you track your feelings and monitor your thoughts. Writing gives you an outlet for your worries, fears, dreams, and honest conversations. It is an avenue to express yourself without the fear of judgment. When you are honest with yourself through journaling, it helps you learn more about yourself and it helps you acknowledge your feelings (University of Rochester Medical Center, n.d.).

Keeping a journal helps you store your secrets and insecurities. Start by purchasing a compact journal that you can easily carry with you. You can use it to track your thoughts throughout the day. Alternatively, keeping a journal on your nightstand helps you make the process a routine. You can jot down your thoughts before bed or reflect on your day. This option prevents any anxiety about taking your journal out of your home. Similarly, you can opt for a digital journal on a tablet or your cell phone. It is a convenient method to track your thoughts because we always have our devices. I enjoy writing in a physical journal because it adds to my routine and puts my thoughts in one place. I can easily revisit entries and track my development. This exercise is an easy way to reduce your stress and helps you understand your emotions. The task forces you to develop mindfulness and patience (Bailey, 2018). It helps you access and strengthens the right side of your brain by increasing your creativity.

I suggest journaling daily. It adds routine to your day and helps you reflect on your day. Your journal entry is a personal account of your experiences. Be honest with yourself by writing your genuine thoughts. When you reread your entries, it gives you a new perspective on your experiences. Additionally, it helps you identify the areas you have grown and developed. Your entries do not need to follow a specific format or structure. You can write anything from an account of your day, persistent thoughts, or simply a fond memory. Use these journal prompts to get started:

- My favorite memory from my childhood is...
- I remember when...
- Today I learned about...
- My biggest fear is...
- What I want most out of life is...
- I'll never forget the moment I ...
- When I think about my life, I feel...
- I was raised to always...
- I want to be remembered for...
- Today I am grateful for...
- My talents are...
- The last time I cried...
- The last time I felt overwhelmed...
- The last time I was truly happy...
- At this moment I feel...
- I am grateful for...
- My partner makes me feel...

In conjunction with decluttering your mind, clear your physical space. When you live in a crowded space, it causes stress and feelings of anxiety. Your mind is continuously working causing you to feel overstimulated. Take a moment to look around your space and your décor. How have you styled your space and what does it reflect about you? Strive to create a space with adequate lighting, solid colors, and plants. These small changes help you create an inviting space that is free of color. Store away unnecessary goods and limit decorations.

The Importance of Language

The second exercise to train your mind and increase personal development is understanding the importance of language. The language you use impacts your outlook on life, actions, and the goals you set. The language you use is at the center of your goals because you use it to articulate your feelings, thoughts, and desires. It is the way we communicate with others and tell people about ourselves. We underestimate the power of our words and thoughts. When we speak negatively over our lives or dismiss our abilities, we are doing ourselves a disservice. Our power over our lives lies in our language, our internal dialogue as well as the things we say to others.

The language you use is dependent on your thoughts and surroundings. It is influenced by your culture and society. If you grew up in an environment similar to mine, you became accustomed to swearing and crude jokes at a young age. That environment impacted how I expressed my feelings and interacted with the people around me. These influences are in the subtle habits we possess.

The only way you can alter your behaviors is by understanding your current habits. Track your language habits by monitoring your thoughts for a day. Spend the day monitoring your thoughts and conversations. During this process, write down how you speak and think about yourself. Write down everything that comes to mind, from your reactions to a mistake you make to how you talk about your achievements. Do you downplay your abilities or are you proud of your achievements? Similarly, are you honest about your actions or do you exaggerate and make excuses for yourself? Aid the process by keeping these questions in mind:

- When I speak to people, am I honest about my feelings?
- Do I joke about my skills?
- How do I handle my failures?
- Do I show myself kindness?
- Do I take pride in myself and my work?
- Am I comfortable in my skin?
- Do I insult myself?

These questions help you look for negative habits in the language you use. When you speak negatively about yourself, it limits your thinking. Once you have monitored your thoughts for a day, reflect on what you have written. Look out for the different ways you express your masculinity. What language do you use around manhood? Journal about the language you use and the ways you want to change it.

Alter your negative behaviors around language by using the "catch and release" technique. When you have a negative thought, acknowledge it and replace it with a positive one. Explain to yourself why the thought is false. This simple task is an easy way to shift the way you think and speak about yourself. This task shifts your vocabulary and introduces you to another way of thinking.

The words you use impact the man you are and your relationships. Implement positive affirmations and meditation into your routine to shift your language (Williams, 2017). Affirmations are short statements written in the 1st person to encourage a specific behavior. Pick a behavior you want to change and write an affirmation that speaks to the change. Affirmations are a simple way to counteract your negative behaviors around language. Use your inner voice to encourage yourself and reaffirm your abilities. Here are examples of affirmations you can use to shift your language:

- I am a responsible man.
- I am capable and determined.
- I am caring and kind.
- I am a successful man.
- I understand and acknowledge my emotions.

The Importance of Your Memory

Strengthening your memory and challenging your mind to learn new skills helps you experience personal development. Our memories affect our perspective and actions. You remember a moment based on its effect on your life and the way it made you feel. Your senses are attached to your memories and the impact it has on your mind.

Take a moment to think about your favorite memory. Is it connected to a smell, image, feeling, sound, or taste? Your stronger memories influence your current desires and preferences, for instance. When you train your mind to improve your memory it helps you remain connected to your feelings. Your memory is important because it helps you form your identity. Training your memory benefits your mental well-being. This helps you in your development journey because it exercises your brain and creates opportunities for you to prioritize your needs.

A sharp memory helps you in your personal and professional life. It limits your need for electronic reminders or alarms. There are certain dates and moments that are meaningful to you. When you actively encourage your mind to remember these moments you are keeping your memories alive. This makes you more reliant on yourself as opposed to alarms, lists, and reminders.

Improve your memory through brain training games and phone applications. You can train your mind for a few minutes each day, making the process easily accessible and convenient. They train your mind through riddles, puzzles, numerical challenges. Focus all of your attention on the task you are completing. This ensures that your mind is focused on learning. When you focus your attention on one thing, it increases the likelihood of you remembering it.

Think of it this way: You are more likely to remember the score of a sports match if you are watching it without your phone in your hand. When you split your attention, you force your mind to focus on two things at once. It limits your ability to focus on both tasks (Cheery, 2019). Secondly, train your mind with an occasional spot test. Challenge yourself to recite important dates and memories. This helps you remember details and forces you not to rely on your technological devices. Try cooking a meal from memory as opposed to with a recipe or shopping without a grocery list. This is an easy way to keep your mind sharp and stimulated. It is a simple challenge that tests your recall skills (Melone, 2020).

Furthermore, train your mind through physical exercise and healthy eating. The food you consume affects your physical and mental health. When you consume healthy foods, they encourage healthy brain functions. Depending on your fitness level, start with a walk around your neighborhood or visit the gym. This helps reduce your stress and improves your overall well-being. Once these become habits, it improves your mood and your self-esteem. You become more comfortable in your skin and feel in charge of your body. This feeling of control will motivate you to grow in other areas of your life.

Lastly, train your mind by challenging yourself to learn a new skill. Pick something that you are interested in but have never had the time to try. Do not be afraid to step out of your comfort zone and try something new. It is beneficial to select an activity that teaches you a new skill. When you learn a new skill, it improves your confidence and self-esteem. Here are examples of activities you can include in your routine to challenge your mind:

- build with Legos
- learn a language
- knitting
- constructing puzzles
- solving Sudoku
- completing a crossword
- reading a book
- participating in a woodwork class
- gardening
- playing a team sport

Mental Detox

The final exercise in transforming your mind is understanding the importance of giving your mind a break. Our minds are constantly working or engaged in a task. When we take a break, we often ideally scroll through our phones or watch something on our devices. While these tasks seem relaxing, they limit our ability to give our minds a break. A mental detox allows you to switch off your mind and truly relax. These moments of relaxation allow you to get to know yourself. The same way you would prioritize speaking to a loved one or spending time with them, you need to show yourself the same consideration. Time in your own company allows you to feel closer to yourself.

Start your mental detox with a 24-hour digital break. During this time, you must limit your usage of your technological devices. Put your phone and laptop in a draw or box and challenge yourself to live without them for a day. This task teaches you self-control while forcing you to focus your attention on other areas of your life. A digital detox shows you that you can live without your devices. During this time, take time out to journal and enjoy your own company. Similarly, a mental detox allows you to track your thoughts. Dedicate time to being mindful about identifying negative thoughts and language habits.

Furthermore, detox your mind through a physical detox. When you detox your body from certain foods and beverages, it allows you to clear your mind. Limit your consumption of addictive substances such as alcohol, cigarettes, and junk food. I developed the habit of drinking a beer every day after work while I watched television. It's a simple habit that has become a part of my routine. I realized that I could no longer relax without a cold beer. I needed to reflect on who I was without any other influences.

Setting aside my past habits and reflecting on who I am without added influences helped me understand my motivations and beliefs. My reflections showed me that many of my habits were developed from other men and ideas around masculinity.

Set time aside to reflect on your life and actions. Change your environment by reflecting in your garden or a park. The fresh air helps improve your mood and overall well-being (Wiest, 2018). When you spend time alone, use the opportunity to reflect on your life and character. Get to know yourself. Reflections are moments of contemplation about a specific topic.

Reflect on your life using these prompts:

- What does self-awareness mean to me?
- What does being a man mean to me?
- When I was younger, what were my expectations of manhood?
- Am I proud of the man I am?
- How can I better myself?
- How does spending time alone make me feel?

Reflections show your willingness to learn and develop yourself. Further this growth by joining a support group and associating yourself with like-minded men. Finding people who understand the importance of growth assists you in your development journey. They motivate you to push yourself and commit to the changes you want to see. Similarly, speaking openly about your growth with your friends and family assists other men in understanding the importance of personal development. You help shape one another's perspectives on manhood (Men's Group, 2021).

CHAPTER 5

The Emotionally Intelligent Man

Emotional intelligence is a key component in your development journey. It helps you navigate situations and understand the people around you. Your emotional development is vital because it helps you understand how you feel and the impact of your actions. Emotional intelligence refers to your ability to monitor and understand emotions. This trait helps you manage yourself and the people around you (The Economist, n.d).

This is vital because emotions are at the center of all of our interactions. Emotional intelligence, like any characteristic, can be learned over time. You can develop emotional intelligence if you have a willingness to learn and approach it with intentionality. Emotional intelligence helps you navigate your professional and personal relationships.

Emotional intelligence consists of three key components: perception, consideration, and management (Cherry, 2020). Perception allows you to develop the ability to identify and feel your emotions and the people around you. You must develop the ability to identify different emotions and what they are telling you. This skill helps you interact with different people and perceive social cues. Develop this skill by observing your surroundings before engaging with people. Try to perceive their feelings and take note of their reactions. Ask yourself what their body language is saying about their feelings. Are they open and inviting, or are they closed off? Take note of these distinctive signs in their body language. They help you understand how the person is feeling as well as how you must approach them. Understanding body language helps you monitor your body's behavior. Assess what your body language is saying to the people around you. Does your body language match the feelings you are experiencing? This is the first step in emotional understanding, because it marks the start of understanding yourself. Similarly, understand that your emotions are complex. You can feel more than one thing at a single time.

The second component is consideration. Consideration refers to your ability to be mindful of another person's feelings. When you are considerate, it increases your awareness of someone's feelings and assists you in developing empathy (Cherry, 2020). Be mindful of your reaction to an individual by showing kindness and understanding. Similarly, when you are considerate of your feelings, it assists you in developing as an individual. Give yourself the freedom to feel and understand your emotions.

When you successfully identify your emotions, accept what you are feeling by showing yourself empathy. An aspect of emotional intelligence is your ability to acknowledge your emotions and react despite them. This skill helps you in professional and personal spaces. Do not allow yourself to be led by your emotions or momentary feelings. Understand the importance of acknowledging the emotion and its origin. Take this approach to your emotions and the emotions of others. When the people around you are behaving in a way that you do not understand, acknowledge their feelings and their origin. This helps you gain perspective and understand their emotions when you react. This creates a space for healthy communication in your relationships. Strive to show consideration in every area of your life.

Management is the final component of emotional intelligence. Once you have successfully perceived and understood your emotions, you must decide how you manage the feeling. The management of your emotions influences how you are perceived and understood. Consider this example: You are in an argument with your partner. During this disagreement, you try to express the issues in your relationship. If you convey your feelings in an angry tone, your partner focuses on your emotion as opposed to the cause. If you acknowledge that you are angry, you can move past the feeling and constructively express yourself. This is an example of successfully managing your emotions. Management helps you develop the ability to behave correctly in all situations (Cherry, 2020). You understand the importance of thinking before you react to a situation.

The Importance of Emotional Intelligence for Men

Developing emotional intelligence is vital for men because it is a skill that is not usually taught. You know as well as I do that emotional intelligence is not encouraged among men. We are told to ignore our emotions and disregard our feelings. This limits our emotional development and understanding. When we do not give ourselves the opportunity to develop emotional intelligence, it causes stress and negatively impacts our mental health.

Emotional intelligence is a part of managing your thoughts and mind. Your emotional intelligence develops from self-awareness and transparency. These traits help you navigate every interaction and action. This is vital for men because it helps them acknowledge their emotions and make decisions from a place of understanding. This helps men show compassion.

Compassion is not a weakness because it helps you acknowledge the humanity in each person. When you approach people from a place of compassion, it gives you a clearer understanding of the situation. This helps you know how to react and behave. It does not change your reaction, but rather, it changes the delivery of your reaction.

When you approach someone from a place of compassion, they are more willing to interact with you. This helps both your professional and personal relationships. Additionally, it helps the way you interact with yourself.

When I was younger, I was trapped in the mindset that men must always hide their emotions and present a tough exterior. I lived this way throughout my teen years and into young adulthood. I hid my feelings and encouraged those around me to do the same. When I learned the importance of emotional intelligence, it gave me the confidence to present my true self to those around me. I felt empowered to live authentically and embrace how I was feeling at any point in time. My emotions helped me see my shortcomings and develop self-awareness.

Emotional intelligence helps you interpret and understand social cues. This understanding helps you navigate different circles. Social cues refer to your body's unspoken indicators, mainly body language and facial expressions. Similarly, understanding the importance of *how* people say things, as opposed to *what* they say, helps you differentiate between different tones. Identify this distinction by asking yourself whether what the person is saying matches how they are saying it (White, 2020). This helps you react accordingly as opposed to misinterpreting people's actions. This understanding helps you develop healthy relationships and interactions.

When you limit your emotional development, it negatively affects your self-image and your relationships with others. Emotional intelligence helps you understand yourself and interact with people genuinely. Create authentic energy around yourself through emotional intelligence. It is essential for men because it teaches you the importance of self-regulation and patience (Carroll, 2020). These skills help you carry yourself and develop healthy relationships. You display emotional intelligence by using your emotions to motivate and empower the people around you. This intelligence helps you interact with a wide variety of people. Emotional intelligence helps you be open-minded in every situation.

Similarly, learning to listen helps you successfully convey your feelings to others. Learning to listen conveys your confidence to those around you. Listening allows you to notice different social cues and feelings. Give yourself room to listen during your interactions.

Test Your Emotional Intelligence

This test will assess your emotional intelligence through a short quiz and scenarios. The scenarios speak to three areas: emotional intelligence, self-awareness, and temperament. The scenarios reflect real-life situations that you are likely to encounter. Your answers should reflect how you would handle each situation.

Scenario #1

You are at a work function socializing with your colleagues. You find yourself in an uncomfortable conversation with your boss.

After they express their opinion, your boss looks to you for yours. Do you express your opinion regardless of how your boss will react, or do you choose to keep your opinion to yourself? In this scenario, an emotionally intelligent person will assess the situation regardless of how they are feeling. During this interaction with your employer, you should consider the impact of your words and reaction. Reacting from a place of anger will jeopardize your job. If you are emotionally intelligent, you can acknowledge that your boss's opinion is not a reflection of yourself.

Scenario #2

You are in a social setting on a night out with your friends. During your night out, you come across an old friend group and start a conversation. Do you express your opinion simply to be heard, or do you consider the reaction of the crowd? This situation, similarly to the previous one, tests your ability to read social cues. Your reaction should not change depending on the person in front of you. You should work with the understanding that regardless of the person in front of you, your reactions should consider their opinion. Whether it's your boss or a distant friend, you should not share an opinion simply for the sake of speaking. You should consider whether your opinion is offensive or appropriate for the situation.

Scenario #3

When you encounter an individual who is not willing to listen to your opinion or see your perspective, how do you react? An emotionally intelligent person is not swayed by the treatment they receive. In this moment, you should identify their unwillingness and change your tactic. You do not focus on judgment or start to feel defensive. Your ability to acknowledge their unwillingness to learn without it influencing your self-image is vital.

Scenario #4

When you feel overwhelmed, do you turn to negative outlets or succumb to your emotions? In overwhelming situations, you should identify the emotions you are feeling and the root of that emotion. This helps you acknowledge the origin of your emotions and move past them. Take a systematic approach to your feelings and allow yourself to feel the emotion. When you feel the emotion, it allows you to structure your approach accordingly (Mind Tools Content Team, n.d).

These scenarios help you identify your temperament and your level of self-awareness. Your temperament refers to your natural personality and character. Your temperament is seen in the way you usually behave and interact with people. You can identify your temperament by monitoring your behavior and natural reactions. Do you tend to react in a calm manner, or do you lean toward passionately expressing yourself?

Regardless of your natural temperament, you can make changes to your behavior to suit your needs. These adjustments help you develop emotional intelligence. If you are naturally reserved, then challenge yourself to express yourself in the right context. If you are naturally outspoken, then challenge yourself to listen more and react calmly.

Remember that improving your emotional intelligence like any area of your life takes time. It requires you to develop the habit of considering your emotions and those of others. Start each interaction with an understanding that your emotions do not need to govern your reactions. This skill is vital for personal development because it encourages you to push yourself. Check-in with yourself and your feelings to ensure that you are continuously growing. This is achieved through continuous conversations and work.

Try to communicate with a trusted group of friends about your expectations and ideas around emotional intelligence. Learn from them and their understanding of emotional intelligence. Speaking to other men about their experiences helps you navigate your interactions. Similarly, these safe spaces help you understand yourself and gain different perspectives. Once you have laid the foundation for understanding emotional intelligence you need to develop positive habits that assist you in your growth.

CHAPTER 6

Develop Emotional Intelligence

Once you have established a firm understanding of your emotional intelligence, you must actively work toward developing the skill. Emotional intelligence tasks are geared toward developing your intuition, understanding, and temperament. This chapter focuses on two areas of emotional development: your personal growth and your emotional understanding of your partner. Start your development journey with journaling exercises that encourage you to develop emotional understanding.

Your emotional journaling for your personal development relies on your ability to develop transparency and accountability. When you write in your journal, it is an opportunity to identify patterns in your behavior. When you write down your thoughts and reflect on what you have written, it helps you look at yourself from another perspective. Read your journal from a place of objectivity. Emotional journaling is an effective way to freely express yourself. It differs from the journaling discussed in chapter four because it is geared toward your feelings as opposed to your mindset. It is effective because it forces you to look at your feelings.

This is a unique opportunity for many of us to consider our emotions for the first time in our lives. In my twenties, I ignored my feelings and focused on what I thought was expected behavior. This affected me when I reached my thirties because I realized that I was unable to form healthy relationships. I brushed aside my feelings and limited my development. Emotional journaling helped me tap into my emotions and develop healthy ways to express my emotions. Additionally, it helped me develop accountability.

Journaling will help you gain perspective and assess your behavior. Use each prompt to write a short entry expressing how the question makes you feel. (Tartakovsky, 2020) Take a moment to use the following journal prompts:

- When I experience strong emotions, it makes me feel...
- Talking about my feelings makes me feel...
- I understand the importance of reading people's expressions...
- I react to different personalities by...
- I handle discomfort by...
- When I am uncertain about my feelings I tend to...
- My ideas around emotional expression are based on...
- If I offend someone, I react by...
- I try to understand my emotions by...
- When I am unable to understand my emotions I rely on...
- A healthy way to show my emotions is by...
- When someone's words do not match their feelings, I feel...
- To express my emotions, I must feel...
- I trust my emotions when...
- I have emotional scars about...
- I feel deeply affected when...

Relationships

- When my partner is experiencing strong emotions, I start to...
- When my partner experiences sadness, I react by...
- During an argument, if I feel confronted, I react by...
- My fighting style is...
- Do my feelings about my partner match how I treat them?
- What do I do to negatively affect my partner's emotions?
- How does my partners' reaction to my emotions make me feel?
- Do I feel like my partner considers my emotions?

In addition to your journal entries, explore and develop your emotional intelligence through bullet journaling. Bullet journaling is a habit-tracking activity that helps you organize your life and track your behaviors. It helps you channel your creativity and manage your day.

Start your bullet journaling process by purchasing a compact journal. Dedicate each page to monitoring your day. Track your emotional intelligence by writing down your emotions. Similarly, you can use the journal to create other positive habits to help your personal development. Note each habit with an illustration or rating. Answer the following questions each day to help you monitor your emotions:

- How am I feeling today?
- How did I manage my emotions today?
- What trait can I work on?
- Did I express my feelings?
- Did I understand my feelings?
- Start a mood tracker.

Reflections and Invitations

Use the following invitations and reflections to develop your emotional intelligence. Choose a quiet place where you can focus on your reflection and spend time developing yourself without any distractions. The reflections are aimed at helping you review your current thoughts and behaviors. Use them as an opportunity to track your growth and continuously map your development. This is achieved by reviewing your answers monthly. It helps you remember the steps you must take toward growth. Consider the following reflections and invitations:

- Imagine yourself in a healthy, happy relationship. What does this relationship add to your life, and how does it make you feel?
- You are stranded on a deserted island with your partner. What will be your biggest disagreement and biggest strength?
- I invite you to reflect on the emotions you often fear. Ask yourself why the emotion scars you, how you navigate it, and how you hope to develop it.
- Imagine yourself 10 years from now sitting in your home. What is one thing you hope to have learned by this stage?
- Imagine yourself 10 years from now sitting in your home. Reflect on one trait you hope you have left in the past?
- What does my relationship mean to me, and why is it important to me?
- I value these emotions... because...
- My understanding of love languages is...
- Take a moment to describe where you are and how you are feeling.

Once you have reflected on your answers, write development goals that are geared toward your growth. If you notice that you lack tact and self-awareness, create goals to encourage this development. Additionally, I suggest you format your goals similarly to your affirmations. Make them short, direct, and intentional (Aya, 2020). If you struggle with self-awareness and tact, these are examples of goals you can create:

- I am capable of expressing myself productively.
- I accept my emotions and strive to understand them.
- I am conscious of the effect of my words.
- I must be accountable for my actions.
- My actions match my emotions.
- I express my emotions in an honest way without offending those around me.
- I understand social cues.
- I assess facial expressions and words before expressing myself.
- Every day I develop in my growth journey.
- I approach my feelings from a place of understanding.
- I am a man who understands the importance of self-awareness and tact.
- I understand the man I am and am confident in that.
- What moment makes you feel proud of yourself?
- Write a letter to your younger self reflecting on your life.
- Write down the highlights and lowlights of your life?
- My behavior is impacted by my ability to…
- Write a letter to your past trauma.
- Write a letter to a person who has hurt you explaining what they have done and how it made you feel. Additionally, acknowledge the role you played in the situation.
- Are you your authentic self?
- Can you freely express yourself when you are around new people?

- Am I content with my life?
- What areas of my life would I change to allow myself to live authentically? (Ackerman, 2021)

Quick Check-Ins

Daily

- How am I feeling today?
- Best moment?
- Overall mood?
- Worst moment?
- Tomorrow I hope for...

Weekly

- This week I achieved...
- The highlight of my week was...
- The lowlight of my week was...
- This week I felt...
- Next week I want to achieve...

Monthly

- This month I felt...
- The highlight of my month was...
- The lowlight of my month was...
- If I could change one thing about my month, it would be...
- Next month I want to develop in this area...

Annually

- Did I live authentically?
- Did I prioritize my emotions?

- Did I prioritize my mental health?
- How am I feeling about my overall year?
- Did I achieve the growth I set out to?

CHAPTER 7

Spiritual Growth

Spiritual growth is the next area you must focus on for your personal development. Spiritual growth refers to your ability to find yourself and develop as a person. You can discover your soul and seek a state of harmony with your body, mind, and spirit. When you discover yourself in this manner, it helps you feel at peace. This sense of peace helps you live freely and authentically. You no longer seek validation from outside sources like your friends, family, and career. This development helps you continuously grow and find yourself as a person. Spiritual growth is considered every step you take toward your development. Regardless of the size of your development or progress you make, it adds to your development.

Start each day seeking to develop yourself and discover a new aspect of yourself. When you give yourself the opportunity to discover more about yourself it opens your mind to new possibilities. This development helps you stay interested in your life and continuously excited about your potential. Your spirituality is not linked to any form of organized religion or spiritual expectations. Give yourself the freedom to develop in ways that are unique to you. This chapter will further explore spiritual growth, development, and discovery that assist you in your journey.

Spiritual growth is vital for men in their development journey. It assists them in self-expression and discovery. Keep in mind the individuality that lies in self-discovery. Your expressions of spirituality are different from the next person's because of your personality and spirit. Spirituality helps you understand yourself better and navigate through the daily challenges of your life. When you are spiritually sound, it gives you a place to draw from and seek guidance.

The key to your spirituality is about feeling connected to your intuition and seeking guidance with yourself. You are the only person who understands your experiences and desires. When you trust your instincts, it gives you the confidence and motivation to seek out different parts of yourself. Give yourself the freedom to seek out a deeper understanding in every area of your life. This is vital for men because it gives us an opportunity to express ourselves.

Oftentimes spirituality is indeed associated with femininity and deep emotions. This is not an area that men are expected to explore. We are celebrated in organized religion but not seen in spirituality. Additionally, spirituality carries many stereotypes and unfair associations. If you are spiritual, you are associated with long hair, a nomadic lifestyle, recreational drugs, and a lack of stability. This is not the case as spirituality suits all lifestyles and people. Express your spirituality in a way that suits you while you push yourself out of your comfort zone. My spiritual exploration helped me discover different areas of my life. In my circles, I found that men were not comfortable discussing spirituality because they associated it with femininity. Spiritual growth is vital for us because it helps us discover new areas of our lives and emotions. It should not be associated with femininity because these are traits that are universal (Simonova, 2020).

There are different areas of spirituality that you can explore. The first area is referred to as *inner spiritual growth*. This type of spiritual growth focuses on listening to your inner voice and instincts. Your ability to rely on yourself motivates you to develop yourself and your instincts. Furthermore, this form of spirituality helps you feel connected to the people around you. You acknowledge that each person has a spirit that requires nurturing. This makes you feel closer to each person you meet and empathic to his or her experiences. Inner spiritual growth helps you familiarize yourself with your emotions and develop a deeper understanding into what being a man means to you. This process helps you shape and redefine the expectations you set for yourself by encouraging you to believe in what you have to offer the world. Your strength comes from accepting yourself and your true essence. Discover yourself through inner reflection and meditation.

Practical spirituality is the second form of growth you can achieve. Practical spirituality refers to your ability to develop your spiritual side through your mental stimulation. You value practical thinking and fact over fiction. If something is a proven fact, it holds weight in your life. When you seek guidance you turn to tried and tested theories. You seek advice from people who have experienced similar situations. You are a practical thinker who believes that the answers you seek have practical explanations. Developing new theories and ideas helps you discover more about yourself. It helps you live confidently because it brings you closer to discovering more about yourself. You are open to experiencing different thoughts and opinions because you believe it brings you closer to yourself. Practical spirituality is useful because it relies on your ability to seek out knowledge. You are only limited by your desire (Simonova, 2020).

The third type of spiritual growth is achieved through *organized religion* (Simonova, 2020). If you believe in organized religion, dedicating yourself to a specific religion helps you feel grounded. Organized religion is suitable for people who need routine and guided growth. Organized religion typically gives followers specific rules and expectations about their behavior. In this type of spirituality, you are offered guides to turn to for direction. The different readings direct your actions in each area of your life. If you are struggling with a specific area in your life, you can turn to the text for guidance. This helps people feel supported and brings meaning to their lives.

Additionally, organized religion places you in a social setting where you can encounter like-minded people. This helps you in your growth because it allows you to seek guidance. Your expressions of spirituality are dictated by the religion of your choice. This is a popular solution for the growth of many. This type of religion gives people a higher power to believe in as they seek to believe in a higher purpose. Organized religion is based on the belief that each person has a purpose and they can turn to spiritual guidance for assistance.

Additionally, you can express your spirituality through the kindness and generosity you show to others. Kindness and generosity is an act of spiritual growth because it helps you help the people around you. When you show kindness you are acknowledging that humanity is an important aspect of human existence. This type of spiritual growth helps you feel connected to the people around you through thoughtfulness.

Men are typically not praised for kindness or generosity. When you explore this area you are allowing yourself to express your emotions. When you offer people kindness without the expectations of reciprocity, you are expressing your genuine nature. This act goes against what we are taught as men and more importantly as people. You only involve yourself in situations that later benefit you. Go against this idea by developing your spirituality through kindness and generosity (Simonova, 2020).

Lastly, express your spirituality through meditation and physical tasks. This form of spiritual growth helps you feel physically connected to your body. This connection to your body helps you express your emotions and manage your thoughts. The spiritual connection is the bond that develops between your body and mind. This connection develops your confidence and helps you manage your stress. Select an activity that suits your lifestyle. The physical activity you select can be anything from yoga, weight lifting, running to swimming. It helps if you try different tasks until one suits your body. Meditation in conjunction with this physical sport helps you find a moment of pause in your routine.

Meditation is a moment of contemplation and reflection that you can use to understand yourself. It is an opportunity for your mind to focus on one area of your life. Use your spiritual meditation to focus on the areas you want to develop. In your spiritual journey, this meditation should seek to develop your understanding of others and your overall behavior. Meditate on your mind, emotions, spirit, and personality.

Key Terms in Spiritual Development

Your spiritual growth is assisted through four key concepts. These terms help you gain perspective and a genuine understanding of yourself. Your spiritual growth does not need to be directly connected with religion. This gives you room to express your spirituality through alternative routes. These four concepts help you develop spiritual growth and connections. We will explore the importance of each trait and how it helps you as a man. Keep in mind the importance of keeping an open mind. It will assist you in understanding the importance of each trait in the current stage of your life.

The first concept is *positivity*. Positivity is your ability to look at situations preferably. Positivity helps you reflect on negative situations and seek favorable outcomes. This shift in your perspective is vital in your development journey. When you shift your perspective, you are changing your outlook on your current situation. Seek out optimism in every area of your life. When you develop this ability, it helps you manage stress, seek happiness, and live freely. Positivity helps you feel encouraged and supported. This helps you in your spiritual growth because it helps you develop something you can rely on. It is a key concept because it helps you shift your mindset. Once you develop a positive mindset, it helps you show yourself empathy and compassion.

Positivity helps you cultivate beneficial behaviors and habits. These habits are shifting how you manage your emotions, thoughts, and behaviors. It helps you learn the importance of giving yourself moments of joy. This is essential in your spiritual development journey because it helps you feel connected to yourself and your spirit (Davis, n.d). True positivity helps you overcome the difficulties that come with manhood. It gives you the support to encourage yourself when you face adversity. Positivity benefits you by improving the quality of your life by improving your physical and emotional well-being.

The second concept is *abundance*. Abundance in your spiritual development journey refers to your ability to create a fruitful rich life for yourself. This richness helps you feel connected to your spirit and further develop your identity. Believing in an abundance mindset helps you shift your perspective. An abundance mindset is the belief that you can create the life you imagine for yourself. You believe in your capabilities and your desire to better yourself. When you develop an abundance mentality, you carry yourself with authentic confidence. It helps you lean into your spirituality by allowing you to explore yourself. An abundance mentality helps you handle adversity and manage change. Every person overcomes these natural shifts in their lifetime. An abundance mentality is about celebrating your ability to create the life you desire regardless of your circumstances. It helps you acknowledge that you are a capable individual (Goguen, n.d).

The next concept to develop is *gratitude*. Gratitude helps you create room for positive space in your life. Gratitude relies on your ability to show kindness and understanding to the people around you. You openly express your thankfulness to the people in your life. You can express gratitude for every area of your life, from your relationships, career to your belongings.

Gratitude in relation to your spiritual development helps you develop peace around who you are and what you own. When you display gratitude, you are allowing yourself to display deep appreciation. Additionally, gratitude is experienced as a genuine appreciation that feels like a deeper emotion. This emotion helps you acknowledge the blessing in your life. These blessings stem from your inner and external blessings. When you develop the ability to express appreciation for your inner blessings it helps you feel confident and content.

The second area of gratitude that you can explore is your physical belongings. The key is to develop a balance between your gratitude toward your physical belongings and blessings.

Do not allow yourself to fall into a materialistic mindset. Your gratitude is not based on what you own but rather what the item means to you. Gratitude is a key concept in your spiritual growth because it is an act of selflessness (Ackerman, 2022). Showing gratitude makes you happier and reduces your stress. Additionally, gratitude results in better sleep, relationships, and health. This is possible because of the peace gratitude brings you (Holland, 2019).

The final component is *manifestation*. Manifestation in your development journey refers to your ability to create the life you desire. Manifestation is sometimes associated with incantations and magic, but this is not always the case. Manifestation is your ability to better yourself to reach your goals. When you achieve your personal development goal, you better your chances of improving yourself in every area of your life. The work you put into your development puts you in a position to accept and receive new opportunities. The non-tangible aspect of manifestation that is associated with magic is your ability to attract the life you desire. Use this attraction to cultivate positive behaviors in yourself that will attract the life you desire. Manifestation functions on your ability to commit to your goals and seek your desires. You cannot overlook the effort that you put into drawing your desires to you (Zapata, 2020).

CHAPTER 8

Spiritual Growth Exercises

Once you understand the foundation for spiritual growth, you must assess where you are in your journey. This assessment gives you perspective and helps you set your spiritual growth goals. Spiritual growth takes shape in different forms, depending on your beliefs and desires. You do not have to believe in a specific religion or ideals, but rather, you must create habits that work for you. I will share various spiritual practices with you that helped my development. Feel free to adjust each task to suit your needs. Spiritual growth is meant to propel your understanding of yourself. Each task should speak to a goal you have set for yourself and a behavior you want to expand. It helps you feel at peace in every area of your life.

The Test

Start your growth journey by taking the following test. This test will assist you in identifying where you are in your journey.

- Do I consider myself a spiritual person?
- How do I define spirituality?
- What areas do I want to develop?
- What are my current spiritual practices?

- What worries me about spirituality?
- Do I consider myself a compassionate person?
- Do I consider myself an intuitive person?
- Do I enjoy believing that there is something bigger than me?
- Do specific structures in my day and life make me feel supported?
- Do I enjoy feeling connected to the people around me?

Each question sheds light on your spirituality. There is room for development for each person on their journey. Non-religious spiritual practices are an effective way to grow your spirituality. We will explore the different ways you can develop your spirituality. Each task benefits you by creating opportunities for you to grow and discover yourself. The positive habits you develop help you add structure to your day and emphasize with the people around you. Spirituality helps you feel content and happy in your life.

Developing Your Spiritual Growth

You can develop your spiritual growth through the following activities. We will divide the activities into the four key concepts we discussed in the previous chapter: Positivity, Abundance, Gratitude, and Manifestation.

Develop Positivity

Create positivity in your life through positive thinking and behaviors. When you start your day with positivity, it carries into your day. The aim is not to lie to yourself but to develop the ability to see the good in each moment.

When you wake up every day, look for one thing to be excited about in your life. Looking for moments of joy and excitement helps you develop genuine excitement for your day. Shift your mind away from your negative thoughts and learned behaviors. This shift happens when you allow yourself to look for the good in your life. The aim is to start seeing the world through rose-tinted glasses. The aim isn't to develop naivety or lie to yourself but to learn an appreciation for your life. Often as men, we allow ourselves to develop a self-critical mindset. Positive self-talk directly contradicts this habit by challenging us to see the positive in ourselves.

Secondly, you can develop positivity by surrounding yourself with positive images and messaging. Positive images keep you motivated and inspired. Select images that speak to your interest. This helps you create a space that is inviting and beneficial for your life. Surround yourself with positive quotes that speak to your insecurities and encourage you. This helps you develop a positive mindset and approach to your life (Davis, n.d).

Develop positivity by volunteering your time. When you volunteer your time, it brings you closer to spirituality by pushing you into a selfless task. Volunteering gives you a new perspective and helps you better yourself. Pick an interest and cause that speaks to you. Volunteering helps you feel fulfilled and happy. The joy you experience leaves you feeling valued and needed. Additionally, when you volunteer, it opens your mindset to the needs of others. It helps you treat people with empathy and understanding.

Lastly, create positivity by learning the importance of release. When you experience a negative emotion, thought, or behavior you must learn to release it. Similarly to catch and release in fishing, learn to catch and release negativity. When you find yourself in these situations, acknowledge the thought and release it back into the world. It helps you acknowledge your emotions without allowing them to govern you. Once you have developed emotional intelligence, it becomes easier to manage your emotions. Practice the catch and release technique in every area of your life.

Develop Gratitude

Develop gratitude by dedicating an area of your journal to gratitude entries. Setting aside space for a gratitude section within your journal helps to commit to journaling and bettering yourself. This area helps you keep track of each day of your life. Create gratitude entries by committing a section of your journal to track your thoughts. Write each date followed by the moment that made you feel grateful. You can write about any moment in your day regardless of how small or large it is. The section aims to give you perspective on each day. When you read the entries at the end of the year, it gives you perspective on what you have experienced. Alternatively, use the section weekly to write down the highlights of that week. This helps you develop gratitude without requiring your daily attention (Holland, 2019).

Secondly, develop gratitude by surrounding yourself with positive influences. The things you surround yourself with and consume affect your outlook on life. When you surround yourself with positive influences it helps you develop gratitude. This helps you use positive words and surround yourself with positive people. They help you feel encouraged and supported by the people around you. The positive influences around you help you appreciate the things around you. When you begin to view your current environment with different eyes, it helps you develop gratitude.

Start writing a weekly thank you note to yourself. A weekly letter to yourself is an easy way to acknowledge what you do and how you are feeling. The letter can vary in length, but it needs to cover what you are grateful to yourself for achieving. Take a moment to express your gratitude by giving yourself a moment to show yourself compassion. The letters are specifically vital for men because they are an opportunity to show yourself kindness. It is a moment of vulnerability for you, and it helps you acknowledge your emotions. Additionally, you can write a letter to another person or jot down an abstract idea. It is an effective way to show yourself your appreciation for the things in your life (Holland, 2019).

Further, develop gratitude through mindfulness activities like meditation and purposeful activities. Meditation is an opportunity for you to focus on one aspect of your life at a time. It helps you separate yourself from the different areas of your life. Develop gratitude by dedicating each time for meditation to one area of your life. When you focus your energy on one area of your life, it helps you appreciate it. Meditate on areas of your life you want to improve (Holland, 2019).

Develop Abundance

Developing an abundance mindset, similarly to practicing manifestation, requires you to trust in yourself and your goals. When you start your goals with an abundance mindset, it helps you focus on achieving those goals. You must trust in the goals you have set for yourself as well as the possibility of the future goals you will achieve. This helps you continuously develop yourself and propel yourself to achieve your future goals. Abundance inspires you to seek more out of your life. Further, develop your mindset by giving yourself room to make mistakes and grow. When you create goals you should not limit your mind to the goal. Allow the goal to grow and develop with you.

Develop an abundance mindset by changing how you view and navigate your life. Shake off the belief that you will fail and the changes you take will not be successful. Developing an abundance mindset helps you live confidently. It helps you change your perspective and view your current situation in a beneficial way. When you face adversity it helps if you view it as a learning experience as opposed to a setback. Use the situation to feel empowered and in control of your life.

An abundance mindset also helps you appreciate your life and position. Every time you achieve something, use it as an opportunity to develop your confidence. Acknowledge how far you have come and developed in your life. This development assists you in pinpointing moments of success in your life.

Take a moment to reflect on your past and the different ways you have developed over the years. Look at the differences between how you behaved five years ago compared to how you behave now. Looking at your behavior in your twenties helps you see different behavioral patterns and habits. Develop your confidence by acknowledging how far you have come. This helps you notice the abundance in your life. Abundance is not about your finances; rather, it is a moment to appreciate the abundance in your life. This is anything from an abundance of ideas, people, and feelings to personality traits.

<u>Develop Manifestation</u>

Practice manifestation by creating a vision board. A vision board is a physical or digital collage that represents everything that you desire. You place relevant images and words that represent your desires. Start by creating a list of goals and selecting an image or word to represent the respective goal. It helps you remember your desires and work toward your goals. When you achieve a goal, place a tick next to the item. This helps you track your progress and manage your productivity. Vision boards help you manifest your desires by serving as a reminder of the work that you need to put in to reach each goal. Do not limit your mind to the goals you have set. When you create a vision board, do not limit your mind to what you see daily. Feel free to create goals that are relevant to each phase of your life. Add to your vision board and adjust your goals as you see fit. This makes room for you to adjust as you develop as a person (Zapata, 2020).

Secondly, practice manifestation by creating a manifestation journal. In conjunction with your vision board, create a list of affirmations to assist you in your journey. The list outlines and helps you define your goals. When you learn to articulate your goals, it helps you devise a strategy to achieve them. In your journal, write notes on each goal. If your goal is to receive a promotion in your job then write notes to the goal that speaks to that goal.

This is an example of notes you can write to this specific goal. "I will receive a promotion in the next six months. I deserve this position because of my ability to…" "My work as a ____ helped me receive my promotion." And lastly, "This promotion helped me better myself by achieving____." These examples of notes help you manifest your goals by visualizing them.

When you write down a goal, make sure that you start to live in a way that creates room for the goal. If you aim to receive a promotion then adjust your behavior to accommodate that goal (Lorie, 2021). Achieve your desires by surrounding yourself with positive energy and an upbeat attitude. The attitude you carry into your daily life influences your ability to manifest. When you create your goals, have a positive attitude and live with the knowledge that you *will* achieve your goal. The key is to believe that you deserve to reach your goal. Creating an environment and attitude that creates space for your desires helps you achieve your goals.

Lastly, develop your spirituality through manifestation by learning to trust yourself (Guerin, 2017). When you start your manifestation process, you must trust yourself and your ability to reach your goal. When you create your list with the understanding that you trust yourself it motivates you to achieve your goals. You must trust in yourself and your life to help you achieve your goal. The trust you have for yourself builds your confidence and furthers your desire to achieve your goals.

Journaling Prompts for Spiritual Development:

Positivity

- I love x about my life.
- When I am feeling down I turn to...
- My happiness comes from...
- I am most positive when I...
- I am the best version of myself when I...

Abundance

- I have an abundance of x in my life.
- My proudest achievement is...
- I enjoy helping people by...
- What does abundance look like for me?
- How have your ideas around abundance changed over time?

Gratitude

- Today I am grateful for...
- I appreciate my ability to...
- Today I expressed gratitude by...
- What excites me about my life?
- Thankfulness is important to me because...

Manifestation

- I will achieve...
- My desire is to...
- My confidence comes from...
- I will achieve the life I desire by...
- My dedication comes from my...

Use this space to write your spiritual practices

CHAPTER 9

Tri-Dimensional Inner Growth

You have pushed and challenged yourself along this journey. I am sure by now it has become clear that personal growth is about honesty and a willingness to work. We have explored various areas of your life to help you develop as a man. It takes courage to admit that you require assistance and guidance, especially in your 30s. These are the years we are expected to be living confidently. There is not any space for exploration or discovery. This limits our development and further limits our lives. We have traveled on a journey throughout this book.

Looking at your mental, emotional, and spiritual growth, we've examined the key areas that are pivotal for change to occur, namely our mindset, emotional intelligence, and spiritual growth. These areas are vital in our development because they represent our personalities and key habits. When you implement effective change in these areas it allows you to develop positive habits.

The mental changes you made in your life required you to understand the power and importance of your mindset. A strong mindset can propel you into the next stage of your life. It helps you identify mental slumps and navigate them when they occur.

The aim is to understand your mindset and make changes that increase your self-acceptance and productivity. Similarly, you must shake off the expectations you have of manhood and create your own parameters. You should have created new mental routines and expectations for yourself. This is a key step in your journey because it helps you define your life.

The aim is to have different expectations for your personal and professional life that are unique to you. These changes are strengthened by your development of resilience, mental toughness, and reflections. They help you prepare for the journey and the change you will make in the other areas of your life. This time should have taught you the control you hold over your life.

During this stage of your development, you learned the importance of journaling, the importance of language, developing your memory, and mental detoxing. These steps helped you learn the importance of writing and conveying an honest account of your life to yourself. The vulnerability that journaling requires helps you develop as a person. Similarly, this role helps you understand the importance of language in your journey. You must carry with you an understanding of your inner voice, language, and positive thinking. These traits help you develop transparency and understand yourself. You should have developed a firm mental understanding of what you desire. Additionally, training your memory, giving yourself a break, and monitoring your inner and external influences help you develop your mind. Once you develop your mindset, it helps you feel in charge of your life. Remember the fundamental traits you have learned in this phase of your journey. You should see increased mental awareness and confidence within yourself.

Secondly, emotional intelligence is the next component of your journey. In this phase, you explored the importance of perception, consideration, and emotional management. These three factors help you lay the foundation for your emotional intelligence. When you develop the ability to understand social cues, it helps you develop healthy relationships and navigate social settings. This is key to understanding your emotions and the impact of your actions on others. When you develop emotional intelligence it helps you improve your self-esteem and your outlook on life. This is vital for men because it helps us interact with a wide variety of people without limiting ourselves. The test geared toward emotional intelligence helped you examine your position and create goals that helped you develop.

Remember that your emotional understanding guides how you react to people and how they react to you. When you develop your emotional intelligence, you add structure to your day. The journal prompts, reflections, invitations, and check-ins help you grow yourself through intentionality. This stage reiterated the importance of putting time into yourself and exploring your emotions. Vulnerability is still an emotion that is not encouraged in men. The key takeaway from this phase is understanding the importance of your emotions. When you are vulnerable about how you are feeling, it helps you navigate your relationships. This results in stronger emotional connections and an accurate representation of your personality.

Remember to allow yourself the opportunity to continuously explore your emotions. The effects of these exercises should result in your ability to articulate your feelings and express your emotions without apprehension. A key factor is your ability to manage your emotions. Emotional intelligence helps you no longer fall victim to a quick temper or miscommunication. When you allow yourself to pay attention to social cues and unspoken gestures, it helps you feel better equipped to tackle conversations.

The final step in your journey is your spiritual growth. Your spiritual growth helps you balance out your personality and the connection you have with yourself. When you understand the spiritual aspect of your life, you break down your personality. Spiritual growth aims to discover your soul and develop a state of harmony within your mind, body, and soul. This peace helps you feel connected to your spirit and continuously better yourself.

We covered the importance of different types of spirituality and their impact on your personality. These allow you to find a spiritual approach that suits your personality and desires. When you are open-minded about your spirituality, it gives you the space to develop positivity, abundance, gratitude, and manifestation. These are the four key areas that propel your spiritual development. This step helped you navigate the importance of feeling in touch with others. It allowed you to understand the importance of overall kindness and generosity. The work you have done in this phase helps you develop positive habits while understanding the importance of spiritual growth. This type of development helps you live in a state of harmony and a deep understanding of yourself.

Your Next Step

Your next step in your tri-dimensional inner growth is to take every skill you have acquired in the respective steps to propel yourself forward. This helps you continuously better yourself and keep developing better habits. It is up to you to decide on the type of man you work toward becoming daily. It is up to you to stick to your habits and continuously allow yourself room to reflect and grow.

Once you have allowed yourself to experience genuine tri-dimensional growth, it is your opportunity to further yourself. Learn to rely on the people around you and allow each other the opportunity to help one another develop. When you surround yourself with an effective support system, it gives you the opportunity to share your experience. Create supportive spaces that challenge your thinking and allow you to be honest. When you learn from the experiences of others, you gain perspective and use the lessons others have learned to better your approach.

Take an active approach at forming positive habits by using these strategies:

- *One task at a time:* This approach is geared toward people who excel by focusing their attention on a single task at a time. It helps you put all of your attention into a single task as opposed to limiting your exploration. When you focus on a task, it gives you an opportunity to see whether it suits your lifestyle. You can slowly adjust the habit to ensure that it works for your routine. In addition, this approach implements behavioral change at the same time each day. If you want to affirm yourself, then practice the behavior at the same time every day. This helps the behavior become a part of your routine (Young, 2021).

- *Twenty-one-day challenge:* This approach requires you to stick to a specific time frame. Committing to this time frame helps you dedicate your time to the change you want to see. Once you commit to this time, it forces you to acknowledge the change and identify whether it meets your needs.

- *Accountability partner:* When implementing a new behavior into your routine, it is helpful to find someone you can rely on to keep you focused on the change. An accountability partner is someone who understands your journey and is dedicated to helping you in your journey. They remind you to commit to your journey. Similarly, they help you feel motivated by reminding you why you are implementing the change. In addition to selecting a trusted person who keeps you motivated, you can select someone who wants to implement a change in his or her life. If you are implementing the same change, it helps you encourage one another. Additionally, it helps you learn from one another as you move through the different stages of your development.

- *Make it easier for yourself:* When you commit to implementing change, simplify the process by making the change easier to achieve. Removing reminders of your past behaviors helps you focus on your change. Consider this example: If you are committing to a healthier meal plan to benefit your overall health, then storing unhealthy items in your home hinders your growth. When you commit to a change, look at your lifestyle and make adjustments that increase the likelihood of your success. This helps you implement a changed behavior into your routine. Changes are effective when you are intentional about committing to the change. It requires your deep desire to live differently (Young, 2021).

- *Reward yourself:* Once you have committed to a change encourage the behavior by rewarding yourself. We all love receiving encouragement or rewards when we show commitment and success in all areas of our lives. Reward yourself when you reach milestones in your journey. This helps you stay committed to the change and helps you stay motivated.

- *Take a break:* Implementing change into your routine can feel overwhelming. When you develop the desire to change your behavior, I discourage overloading your routine with new habits. When you tackle too many new habits, it increases the likelihood that you will not succeed. During the process, ensure that you provide yourself with sufficient time to rest. Taking a break increases your productivity and allows you to be selective about the changes you implement. Breaks are an effective way to ensure that you do not experience burnout or increased anxiety.

- *Baby steps:* The final approach is introducing change into your lifestyle slowly. When you approach change, implementing it into your routine slowly helps you adjust. When you implement small changes in your routine it helps you develop confidence. Your success in the small changes helps you successfully implement larger changes. Additionally, when you set a large goal breaking it down into achievable steps helps you successfully achieve the goal. Consider this example: If you want to learn a new language, then start with basic words and short phrases. Once you have mastered this phase, you can move on to complete sentences and readings. This example illustrates an effective way to start implementing new habits slowly into your routine (Parker-Pope, 2020).

Looking to the Future

When you successfully implement new routines and create lasting change in your routine, it is your opportunity to further your development through new books and development approaches. Further your personal development by reading books that target your insecurities. This tri-dimensional inner growth lays a solid foundation for you to further develop yourself.

Once you have successfully identified your problem areas, it is up to you to further develop yourself. Targeting your problem areas helps you continuously grow. When you focus on these areas you are choosing to leave behind detrimental habits and focus on what you want to achieve. Books introduce you to new ideas and help open up your mind. The perspective you gain helps you select ideas that suit you. When you allow yourself to consider new opinions, it helps you make informed decisions about your growth. Countless self-improvement books and articles tackle issues faced by men. I further my development by taking the time to read short articles weekly. They are an effective way to keep me informed about my personal development. I also enjoy podcasts targeted at men's experiences and helping us develop. When you hear people from different walks of life share their experiences, it helps you create effective habits and new routines.

The final chapter focuses on the importance of journaling for men. While journaling is not a gendered activity, it is typically associated with women. We will explore the different ways that this hinders individual explorations. I am passionate about journaling, especially for men, because it helps us articulate ourselves and our feelings. I will answer every question about journaling and provide you with a practical approach to the activity. It is an effective way to experience real change that forces you to take an honest look at your life.

CHAPTER 10

Revisiting Journaling

Journaling is the simple act of writing; this form of expression is appropriate for all types of writing. Create lists, diary entries, reflections, and expressions that help you make journaling a healthy habit. You should keep journaling because of the countless benefits that it offers. When you journal, it is your opportunity to reflect on your life.

Journals are deeply personal and an opportunity to take an honest account of your life. Additionally, journals allow you to share your deepest feelings and fears with yourself. There is comfort in understanding that your journal is a safe space where you have the opportunity to express yourself. It is a liberating feeling to establish a space that is truly free from judgment and pre-conceptions. This is where the true power of journaling rests. It is a safe space for men that we are not often given.

Consider this example: You have had a bad day and choose to share your experience with a close friend. During this conversation, you notice that your friend seems disinterested and unable to understand your point of view. Once you have finished your conversation, you feel uncomfortable sharing every detail of your experience. You become aware of the shift in your friendship dynamic. Journaling helps you navigate how you are feeling without the fear of judgment. When you journal it helps you learn from yourself. Once you have written an entry, reread what you have written. How do the words make you feel, and what can you learn from them? When you journal you avoid the input of others. If you choose to share your entries with others it is on your terms.

Secondly, journaling is essential because it forces us to be accountable. Accountability is a vital trait for us because it helps us improve ourselves. When you develop accountability it helps you reflect on your actions. Additionally, journaling is an opportunity to implement structure into your routine. When you develop the habit of reflecting on your day it helps identify key areas you should change. It improves your writing and allows you to assess your productivity. This helps you in your professional and personal relationships. Implementing a journal into your routine helps you manage your mental health and stress. You should keep journaling regularly because of the freedom it gives you to express yourself. This freedom helps you stay motivated and encouraged to better yourself as a man. Your personal development relies on your ability to better yourself. The changes you implement into your routine should help you understand yourself without adding increased pressure to your routine. Journaling is a calming task that helps you relax and include moments of reflection into your day.

Journaling Strategies

Start by selecting a medium that works for you. Journaling can take place in physical books and digital applications. The key to successfully journaling lies in your ability to express yourself. The medium you use depends on your lifestyle and routine. A digital journal is effective because it is continuously in your possession. You can journal via your mobile device, laptop, or tablet. When you write in a physical journal, is it a relaxing activity? If you wish to journal at specific times, you must ensure that you travel with your journal. This restricts some of your entries because it does not come with the convenience of a digital journal. When you write in a physical journal it is beneficial to write at specific times. Writing before you start your day or before going to bed is an effective way to create routines (Brown, n.d).

When you write in your journal, use the opportunity to free your mind and write about anything. Starting with a specific structure can limit your thinking. Use your journal as an opportunity to write down the first things that come to your mind. Your journal is your space to express yourself. Write in a way that is authentic to you and your personality. Not every entry needs to be profound and impactful. Every entry is valid and deserves a place in your journal. When you think of men journaling, you may picture flowery language and an overwhelming amount of emotions. This is a valid expectation depending on how you express your emotions but it is not the singular experience (Brown, n.d).

You can openly express your emotions in your journal but if you are not feeling expressive every day you should not force yourself. The aim is to develop an authentic flow in your journal that correctly represents you. When you lack the inspiration to write in your journal, complete a timed writing challenge. A timed writing challenge is simple; you set a three-minute timer and write anything that comes to mind during this time. The timer helps you push yourself to write anything that comes to mind. A timed writing session helps you write about the things that are taking over your thoughts.

Alternatively, you can start your journaling process by writing letters to yourself and the key moments in your life. When you write a letter to yourself it is an opportunity to release emotion. Letters help you express how you are feeling and reflecting on a specific time. I enjoyed writing letters to each year of my life. It allowed me to reflect on the year and give myself an honest account of how I was feeling. The letters serve as a reminder of my achievements and fears.

We have explored numerous exercises to assist your development. Each activity is aimed toward a specific area of development. I will re-introduce the activities we have covered to remind you of the opportunities for growth. When you complete each activity, give yourself room to personalize each task. Your development is assisted through:

- *Journal prompts:* These are short phrases or questions that inspire thoughts, conversations, or writing. They help guide your thoughts by allowing you to focus on a specific topic. Prompts are

- *Reflections:* Scenarios to encourage you to consider different moments you have experienced.

- *Goal creations:* This task helps you create effective goals that meet your needs.

- *Relationship overviews:* This test helps you reflect on your relationship and what you aim to achieve through it.

- *Relationship assessments:* This test helps you acknowledge the role your relationship plays in your life.

- *Five-minute check-ins:* This test gives you five minutes to reflect on your day and experiences.

- *Mental slump detector:* This assessment helps you spot indicators for mental slumps. This helps you avoid these moments and prioritize your mental wellbeing.

- *Language assessments:* This assessment helps you track your thoughts and inner voice. When you assess your language, it helps you consider the way you express yourself. Your language has power over your self-esteem and image. Adjustments to this area help you develop positive habits and increase confidence.

- *Affirmations:* Short phrases to encourage your development in a specific area

- *Training your memory:* Memory improvement activities assist you to develop your thinking and encourage your overall memory.

- *Mental detox:* This activity helps you relax your mind and limit the number of influences around you.

- *Invitations:* These are short prompts that encourage you to reflect on specific topics.

- *Daily, weekly, monthly, and annual check-ins:* These are moments to consider your feelings and thoughts. They help you reflect on a specific period, this assists you in acknowledging your achievements and potential shortcomings.

- *Spiritual development:* Activities directed toward the development of your spirituality through manifestation, abundance, gratitude, and positivity.

Conclusion

I congratulate you for taking this journey with me and exploring your personal development. While I welcome you to the end of this book, this is only the start of your journey.

Real personal growth for men is more than a possibility. It is a key to your continuous self-discovery and exploration. It is your opportunity to tackle any negative habits or behaviors you have ignored in your younger years. Personal development is not limited to a specific area of your life or age.

It is understandable that when you reach your thirties, you start reflecting on the things you need to change. I was in the same position when I turned thirty. I found myself fulfilled in my professional life but unable to navigate my emotions, mental and spiritual spaces. My outlook on personal development shifted when I discovered the importance of prioritizing these three areas.

Understanding the importance of your mental well-being is key in your development. Your mindset sets the pace for your development. We explored the importance of strengthening your mindset through reflections and exercises. These activities helped give you a new perspective and understanding of the power of your mind.

When you allow yourself to strengthen your mind you develop resilience and mental toughness. These traits are vital to creating a fulfilling life. Be mindful of the language you use as it dictates how you view yourself. Give yourself the opportunity to reflect on your favorable traits without limiting your potential. Develop genuine confidence that helps propel you further in your growth journey.

Exploring my emotional well-being helped me navigate my feelings and understand my emotions. Remember that when you allow yourself to explore your emotions, it helps you navigate your relationship. Emotional development helps you develop emotional intelligence. A key takeaway from this book is the importance of emotional intelligence. Continuously remind yourself to remain aware of your emotions and social cues. This helps you navigate different social settings and not rise to every emotion you feel. When you develop the ability to acknowledge your emotions without letting them govern how you live it helps you become a better man.

When I started my journey, defining manhood and masculinity helped me willingly face my feelings. My emotional growth truly happened when I allowed myself to accept my emotions. Journaling and reflecting helped schedule time for my emotional development. I encourage you to set time aside for your emotional development.

Your spiritual growth is the final area that requires your attention. When you connect to your spirituality, you develop understanding and kindness. Growth in your spirituality is beneficial because it helps you understand the experience of others. Allowing yourself to seek positivity, abundance, gratitude, manifestation helps you grow your spirituality. I encourage you to include a spiritual practice in your routine. It will assist you in feeling connected to a different side of yourself.

Every day of your life is an opportunity to better yourself and move further to becoming a better man. Use the foundation you have laid to develop yourself and live authentically. You will always face adversity, but through personal development, you can navigate any situation you encounter.

References

Ackerman, C. (2017, December 18). 87 Self-Reflection Questions for Introspection [+Exercises]. PositivePsychology.com. https://positivepsychology.com/introspection-self-reflection/

Ackerman, C. E. (2017, February 28). What is gratitude and why is it so important? [2019 update]. PositivePsychology.com. https://positivepsychology.com/gratitude-appreciation/

Allegro Media Design. (2021, December 9). What Is Personal Development and Why Is It Important? Www.allegromediadesign.com. https://www.allegromediadesign.com/blog/what-is-personal-development-and-why-is-it-important

Ava. (2016, October 4). 101 Powerful Journal Prompts (+ How to Choose the Right One). Mantelligence. https://www.mantelligence.com/best-journal-prompts/

Bailey, K. (2018, July 31). 5 Powerful Health Benefits of Journaling. Intermountainhealthcare.org. https://intermountainhealthcare.org/blogs/topics/live-well/2018/07/5-powerful-health-benefits-of-journaling/

Brown, C. (2018, April 9). Are You In a Mental Slump? Here Are Six Ways to Get Back on Track. Due. https://due.com/blog/are-you-in-a-mental-slump-here-are-six-ways-to-get-back-on-track/

Brown, G. (2018, June 7). How to Get Into Journaling: The One Thing That Can Change Everything. Primer. https://www.primermagazine.com/2018/live/how-to-journal

Bundrant, M. (2019, January 7). 10 Reasons Personal Growth Is Important No Matter Your Age. Lifehack. https://www.lifehack.org/819331/personal-growth

Carroll, L. (2020, April 14). 5 Signs You're An Emotionally Intelligent Man. Change Becomes You. https://medium.com/change-becomes-you/5-signs-youre-an-emotionally-intelligent-man-5953fbcd6596

Cherry, K. (2019, September 30). Proven Techniques That Really Work to Improve Your Memory. Verywell Mind. https://www.verywellmind.com/great-ways-to-improve-your-memory-2795356

Cherry, K. (2020, June 3). Overview of Emotional Intelligence. Verywell Mind; Verywellmind. https://www.verywellmind.com/what-is-emotional-intelligence-2795423

Davis, T. (n.d.). Positivity: The Psychology, Definition, and Examples. The Berkeley Well-Being Institute. Retrieved February 14, 2022, from https://www.berkeleywellbeing.com/positivity.html

Galla, S. (n.d.). Self Improvement for Men: A Complete Guide to Personal Development. MensGroup.com. Retrieved February 14, 2022, from https://mensgroup.com/self-improvement-for-men/

Guerin, N. (2015, July 20). 7 Steps to Manifest Anything You Want -- Including Money. HuffPost. https://www.huffpost.com/entry/7-steps-to-manifest-anyth_b_7806936

Holland, E. (2019, June 11). 6 Proven Benefits of Gratitude. Chopra. https://chopra.com/articles/6-proven-benefits-of-gratitude

https://www.facebook.com/jamesclear, & Clear, J. (2013, April 11). The Science of Developing Mental Toughness in Health, Work, and Life. James Clear. https://jamesclear.com/mental-toughness

https://www.thesuperiorman.com/author/thesuperiorman. (2014, September 2). The Superior Man. Thesuperiorman.com. https://www.thesuperiorman.com/the-importance-of-personal-development/

Laderer, A. (2019, October 25). How to Get Out of a Slump. Talkspace. https://www.talkspace.com/blog/slump-rut-how-to-get-out/

Melone, L. (2020, June 23). 10 Brain Exercises That Boost Memory. EverydayHealth.com. https://www.everydayhealth.com/longevity/mental-fitness/brain-exercises-for-memory.aspx

Mensgroup. (2022, February 10). Self Improvement Guides - MensGroup.com. MensGroup.com. https://mensgroup.com/self-improvement

Mental Toughness Partners. (2017, October 20). 10 Ways To Build Resilience. Mentaltoughness.partners. https://www.mentaltoughness.partners/build-resilience/

Merriam-Webster. (2019). Definition of RESILIENCE. Merriam-Webster.com. https://www.merriam-webster.com/dictionary/resilience

Mind Tools Content Team. (2009). How Emotionally Intelligent Are You? Boosting Your People Skills. Mindtools.com. https://www.mindtools.com/pages/article/ei-quiz.htm

Parker-Pope, T. (2020, February 18). How to Build Healthy Habits. The New York Times. https://www.nytimes.com/2020/02/18/well/mind/how-to-build-healthy-habits.html

Rolfe, A. (n.d.). Five benefits of personal development. Reed.co.uk. Retrieved February 14, 2022, from https://www.reed.co.uk/career-advice/five-benefits-of-personal-development/#:~:text=Personal%20development%20is%20a%20vital

S, C. (2022). What are social cues. Study.com. https://study.com/academy/lesson/what-are-social-cues-definition-examples.html

Simonova, L. (2020, March 14). 10 Types of Spirituality and Spiritual Practices. Happier Human. https://www.happierhuman.com/types-spirituality/

Staff, M. L. |. (2021, August 20). A beginner's guide to spirituality and manifestation practices. The Daily Californian. https://www.dailycal.org/2021/08/19/a-beginners-guide-to-manifestation/

Tartakovsky, M. (2020, May 27). Journal Prompts to Help You Process Your Emotions. Psych Central.

https://psychcentral.com/blog/journal-prompts-to-help-you-process-your-emotions#1

The economist. (2019). Definition of Emotional Intelligence | What is Emotional Intelligence ? Emotional Intelligence Meaning - The Economic Times. The Economic Times. https://economictimes.indiatimes.com/definition/emotional-intelligence

University of Rochester Medical Center. (n.d.). Journaling for Mental Health - Health Encyclopedia - University of Rochester Medical Center. Www.urmc.rochester.edu. Retrieved February 14, 2022, from https://www.urmc.rochester.edu/encyclopedia/content.aspx?ContentID=4552&ContentTypeID=1#:~:text=Journaling%20helps%20control%20your%20symptoms

Wiest, B. (2018, May 17). 14 Ways To Start A Mental Detox And Declutter Your Mind For Good. Forbes. https://www.forbes.com/sites/briannawiest/2018/05/17/14-ways-to-start-a-mental-detox-and-declutter-your-mind-for-good/?sh=1c49ea956380

Williams, R. (2017, August 11). Why You Should Listen to Your Inner Voice. Chopra. https://chopra.com/articles/why-you-should-listen-to-your-inner-voice

Young, S. H. (2007, August 14). 18 Tricks to Make New Habits Stick. Lifehack; Lifehack. https://www.lifehack.org/articles/featured/18-tricks-to-make-new-habits-stick.html

Zapata, K. (2020, December 22). Exactly How to Manifest Anything You Want or Desire. Oprah Daily. https://www.oprahdaily.com/life/a30244004/how-to-manifest-anything/

www.ingramcontent.com/pod-product-compliance
Lightning Source LLC
LaVergne TN
LVHW051957060526
838201LV00059B/3700